How to Make

A WORLD OF LIQUEURS

by *Heather Kibbey*
and
Cheryl Long

Edited by *Cynthia Fischborn*

First Edition
Copyright © 1983
By Culinary Arts Ltd.
All Rights Reserved

ISBN #0-914667-02-5

TABLE OF CONTENTS

INTRODUCTION 5

BASICS OF LIQUEUR MAKING 7

EQUIVALENT LIQUID MEASUREMENTS 16

MAKING LIQUEURS 17

SERVING AND MIXING LIQUEURS 45

COOKING WITH LIQUEURS 55

INDEX 91

BOOK ORDER FORM 95

ABOUT THE AUTHORS:

Heather Kibbey is a food columnist and freelance writer.

Cheryl Long is the author of the popular companion book, "How To Make Danish Liqueurs", published by Culinary Arts Ltd. She is a culinary instructor and writer.

Both authors live with their families in Lake Oswego, Oregon.

ACKNOWLEDGEMENTS

Our sincere appreciation to our panel of 'expert' tasters, headed by our most dedicated tester, Howard Long: Cynthia Fischborn, Byron Kibbey, Anthony Long, and Jean Ann Randolph.

Special thanks to our Junior Dessert and Food Testers, who served with great enthusiasm, (especially on the dessert-tastings!): Tohren Kibbey, Tristy Kibbey and Michael Long.

We are also grateful to our editor, Cynthia Fischborn; our cover-designer and artist, Marlene King; our Director of Publishing, Jean Ann Randolph; and our manuscript- and proof-typist, Shelley Rogers, for their dedicated and expert help.

INTRODUCTION

This book came about because of the success of HOW TO MAKE DANISH LIQUEURS. Simply, you enjoyed it and wanted more.

This book left Denmark and proceeded to travel around the world, a world filled with famous, even legendary liqueurs. The most difficult part was trying to select which ones to simulate.

To accomplish this somewhat formidable task, a writing partnership was formed. The two of us, as friends and fellow food writers, perceived this as a fun-filled challenge. It was.

It is with a real sense of accomplishment that we present liqueur recipes to you that come as close to duplicating the "great" ones as the limitations of a home kitchen will allow. Most are so close that we suggest a blindfold test of manufactured liqueurs versus our counterparts. Put them in your best decanters and serve or "gift" them with pride.

Our most creative selves came forth on the food recipes. We wanted recipes that were truly worth making and worth remembering, recipes that would not be the same without the liqueurs they were designed for. We enjoyed making them almost as much as our tasters enjoyed evaluating them. We did our share of the tastings too; we each dutifully gained five pounds! Naming each recipe was much like naming our first-born child.

Nevertheless, we made it, enjoyed it and thank you for having requested it. Bon appetit!

Basics Of Liqueur Making

EQUIPMENT:

Making liqueurs at home does not require anything really 'special' in the way of equipment. You will need some, but not all, of the following.

AGING CONTAINERS:

Glass jars with lids (wide mouth, 1-quart or larger best)
Ceramic crock with lid
Ceramic bowls
Glass bottles and/or decanters with either screw-on lids/caps or cork/glass cap

STRAINERS:

Metal colander
Fine wire mesh strainer
Cloth jelly bag
White cotton or linen cloth
Cheesecloth
Paper coffee filters

MISCELLANEOUS:

Wooden spoon
Glass or metal measuring cups
Metal measuring spoons
Metal funnel

PREPARATION OF EQUIPMENT:

The aging containers should be properly cleaned before use. First, wash them thoroughly with a mixture of baking soda and water (approx. 4 Tbsp./dishpanful). The containers should be sterilized by either boiling them in water for

15 minutes or putting them through a full dishwasher cycle without any detergent.

TYPES OF EQUIPMENT:

Kitchen utensils used for liqueur making, such as measuring cups, funnels, etc. should not be made of plastic. (Plastic can impart an 'OFF' flavor to liqueurs.) Metal or glass are preferred.

Straining is one of the most important steps in obtaining a clear, quality liqueur. A large-holed metal colander will strain large pieces but you will need finer straining material for smaller pieces and for your last fine straining. If cheesecloth is used, you will need several thicknesses, which can be discarded after use.

The most efficient fine straining is done with either a cloth jelly bag or with a clean cotton or linen cloth laid inside a strainer. These cloths may be washed and reused. Some prefer to use disposable paper coffee filters for this step, however they are too dense for some of the thicker liqueurs in this book. We recommend that you test a small amount first if you wish to use this method. Try various strainers to see which you prefer.

BOTTLES AND DECANTERS:

You will need an assortment of clean bottles or decanters to hold the finished product. For home storage, wine bottles with metal screw-on tops are frequently the most practical container.

For gift giving, small unusual glass bottles with a metal screw-on top, such as condiment, vinegar and small wine bottles, are excellent.

Glass decanters are elegant containers in which to either serve or give your special liqueurs. Good places to find decanters are garage or rummage sales and second-hand or thrift shops.

Decanters frequently have glass tops with a cork insert. This is fine as long as the cork is clean.

Containers which have held something other than a food or beverage can be difficult to clean and may transfer an offensive or dangerous taste to your liqueur. Therefore, their use is not recommended.

Plastic containers should <u>not</u> be used when making or storing liqueurs. It is also best to avoid all plastic or plastic-lined caps. The reason for this is that the flavor from the plastic can be transferred to the liqueur. The occasional exception is when plastic wrap is laid across a ceramic bowl in the early stages. This is really more of a dust cover and is not used later.

Cork may be used if you wish, but remember that corks allow evaporation. You may wish to seal the cork with wax or foil to avoid this.

INGREDIENTS:

When making any recipe, remember that it is the quality of the ingredients used that determines the final result. There are three main types of ingredients to consider in liqueur making. They are: alcohol, flavorings and water.

ALCOHOL:

There are a number of types of alcohol bases used in liqueur making. The two most frequently used are 180 to 190 proof pure grain alcohol and 80 to 100 proof vodka. Both are easily obtained at your local liquor store.

Pure grain alcohol is a neutral spirit which will be diluted half-and-half with water. It has no taste of its own to interfere with the liqueur flavorings. When purchasing a pure grain alcohol, you do not have to be concerned with which brand to buy; all are equal.

Vodka, like pure grain alcohol, is a neutral spirit usually made from distilled grains. However, there are differences from brand to brand. The purifying and refining processes of the distiller determine the end quality. Good vodka should be colorless, aromaless and have no real taste of its own. In short, it is similar to pure grain alcohol in being an ideal base in liqueur making. Take time to find the 'smoothest' vodka in your price range. Either 80 or 100 proof vodka is acceptable.

The other alcohol bases used in liqueur making are brandy, cognac, American or Irish whiskey, scotch and rum. These all have pronounced tastes of their own and are frequently used with vodka or pure grain alcohol to add their special flavor. Choose them with care and use them sparingly.

Basic brandy is distilled from fermented grape juices. Some brandies are made from other fruits. Avoid fruit-flavored brandies in liqueur making, as they will fight with your flavorings. Choose a good tasting brandy, but avoid the rare, aged and costly brandies which should be enjoyed on their own.

Cognac is a very fine French brandy which derives its name from the area where the wine grapes it is made from are grown, Cognac, France. You may, of course, substitute any brandy for cognac, but when we recommend cognac it is for a superior liqueur.

Whiskey, or 'whisky' as the Scotch and Canadian versions are spelled, is almost as varied in taste as rum. American whiskey is generally distilled from rye, wheat or corn. Irish whiskey and Scotch (short for Scottish whisky) are usually made from malted barley. We have found it best to use Irish whiskey in a traditionally Irish liqueur such as Irish Cream; the flavor is more authentic. Wherever this is important, we have indicated it; if not indicated, use a whiskey that is pleasing to your taste.

Rums are distilled from sugar and molasses. Most are made in tropical countries where the sugarcane grows, most notably the Caribbean. The lighter colored, lighter bodied Puerto Rican or Barbados rums work well. The Jamaican rums are heavier and sweeter. Take care to match the rum to the type of liqueur. Our best advice is to choose a rum that you find smooth and pleasing.

FRUITS, FLAVORINGS & OTHER INGREDIENTS:

Perhaps the most delicate ingredients in liqueur making are the fresh fruits. It does make a difference whether the fruits are picked at the peak of their season or if they are the last stragglers. There really is no substitute for fresh fruit. Sometimes frozen fruit can be substituted, but try to follow the seasons if you can.

In some cases where the fruit peel is used, such as orange peels, either use organic fruit or wash the rind very carefully. Liqueurs can be ruined by a mold, spoilage or spray that is present in the fruit.

Dried fruit liqueurs can be made any time of the year. But again, choose fresh quality dried fruits for best taste. Dried fruits can deteriorate with age but it is a slower process.

Fresh seeds, herbs and spices are frequently called for in our liqueur recipes. We assume, of course, that you will purchase the freshest and best quality possible. While the more common varieties are available in a supermarket, others such as angelica root may not be. Health food stores and herb/spice shops usually carry a wider selection at more economical prices.

In many recipes, a technique called 'bruising' is required. A mortar and pestle are ideal for this technique, however a small bowl and the back of a spoon may be substituted. 'Bruising' is a partial crushing of the seed to release some of the inner flavor to the liquid medium.

Pure glycerine is a thick, clear, colorless liquid available at drug stores, liqueur and winemaking shops, and some herb stores. We think of it as a 'smoothener'. It performs two services: first, it gives additional body to thinner liqueurs that do not have as much natural body as desired. Secondly, it adds a smoothness and slipperiness in the tasting or sipping of a liqueur that speaks of a professional quality. In general, quantities of glycerine will vary, depending upon the need of the individual liqueur. However, we recommend that you do not exceed 1 tablespoon per quart of liqueur.

WATER:

Water quality and taste varies considerably from one area to another. If you have good tasting drinking water, you may choose to use it in liqueur making. However, for the best quality control in liqueur making use distilled water. Distilled water will not impart any off-flavors and you will receive the fullest taste from your liqueur.

AGING:

There is one element in liqueur making that is absolutely essential to good quality and taste: the aging process. We are amazed to find that so many recipes (from other sources) ignore this step. Aging removes the raw edge of the alcohol, no matter which type of alcohol is used. It lends mellowness and a professional quality to a liqueur that develops only with time. Your homemade liqueur will be quite different from its commercial counterpart if not well aged.

We have indicated minimum aging times for each recipe. After this period of time, the liqueur is certainly ready for cooking purposes but you may choose to age it additionally before drinking. We recommend a taste test at this time. Except for the refrigerated liqueurs, most of our recipes will be at their peak after 1 to 2 years' aging.

SIPHONING:

Before the initial straining, most liqueurs have particles of fruit or spices suspended throughout the liquid medium. Careful straining will eliminate these. After aging, other liqueurs, such as our Scottish Highland Liqueur, form a top layer of clear, particle-free liquid over a bottom layer of murky sediment. Attempts to strain this merely result in recombining the two layers, producing a cloudy liquid. Siphoning is a much more efficient way to solve this problem.

Use a piece of plastic tubing 20 to 24 inches long. (Beer and winemaking stores carry tubes especially for this purpose.) Place one end of the tube in the bottle of liqueur so that the end is at a level 1/2 inch above the sediment. Bend the tube and suck gently on the other end until the liqueur fills the tube. With your finger over that end, place it in the empty bottle and at the same time, raise the bottle of liqueur so that the layer of sediment is 4 inches or so above the empty bottle. Release your finger and the liqueur should start flowing from the full to the empty bottle. To stop the flow, just lower the full bottle so that the liquid levels in both bottles are the same. When the clear liquid has been siphoned off, discard the sediment.

BRAND NAMES:

As you leaf through the recipe section of this book, you may find that some of your favorite liqueurs seem to be missing. For instance, you will not see a recipe labeled 'Galliano' because Galliano is the brand name for a specific commercially produced liqueur. Legally, we may not use these brand names for our liqueur counterparts, and so we have invented our own names. (Our facsimile of Galliano is called 'Italian Gold Liqueur'.) Where the name has been changed, we have referred to the original brand name in the italic print at the head of the recipe.

Some names, such as Amaretto and Irish Cream, are not brand names, even though we may associate them with one major producer. For these liqueurs, we were legally permitted to use the familiar title.

EQUIVALENT LIQUID MEASURES

3 teaspoons	=	1 tablespoon
2 tablespoons	=	1 ounce
5-1/3 tablespoons	=	1/3 cup
8 ounces	=	1 cup
16 tablespoons	=	1 cup
2 cups	=	1 pint
16 ounces	=	1 pint
2 pints	=	1 quart
32 ounces	=	1 quart
4 quarts	=	1 gallon
25.6 ounces	=	1/5 gallon or 4/5 quart (known as a 'fifth')
5 fifths	=	1 gallon
1 pony	=	1 ounce
1 jigger	=	1-1/2 ounces
1 dash	=	3 drops
1 milliliter	=	.034 fluid ounces
1 liter	=	33.8 fluid ounces or 4.2 cups
1 fluid cup	=	236 milliliters

Making Liqueurs

DANISH CHERRY LIQUEUR

'Cherry Heering' or 'Peter Heering' as it is now known is a classic ruby-red Danish liqueur with a world-renowned reputation. Our recipe uses dark Bing or other sweet red cherries for a quality liqueur that is amazingly close to this Danish classic.

If you enjoy this Danish fruit liqueur, you may wish to try others from our companion book, 'How to make Danish Liqueurs'. See page 95 for details.

1-1/2 lbs. red cherries with pits, no stems
2 cups granulated sugar
2-1/2 cups vodka
1 cup brandy

Mix vodka, brandy and sugar in a medium mixing bowl. Stir well to dissolve. Cut each washed cherry to open; leave in pits. Place cherries in 2 sterile wide-mouth quart jars or 1 larger container. Pour liquid mixture over cherries and cap with tight lids. For the first two weeks, shake jars several times. Loosen lid after two weeks to check; reseal and let age in a cool place for 3 months, minimum, for best flavor. Strain off liqueur through wire mesh strainer; discard cherries. Rebottle as desired.

VARIATION: For a more prominent 'almond' flavor, pit the cherries. Place cherry pits in a clean cloth and hit with a hammer to break them. Put smashed pits and pitted cherries in quart jars and continue as directed.

# Netherlands

ADVOCAAT

'Advocaat' is a Dutch word which means 'a drink for lawyers'. However, it is not necessary to be a Dutch lawyer to enjoy this mild and velvety egg liqueur.

Unless you have a large capacity blender or food processor, we recommend that you divide the recipe in half and make 2 batches. Makes approximately 1-1/2 quarts.

2-1/2 cups granulated sugar
1-1/2 tsp. vanilla
3/4 tsp. lemon extract
1-3/4 cups vodka

10 whole eggs
2 egg yolks
2 small cans (5.33 oz. each) evaporated milk

Put sugar into blender container or food processor work bowl with steel knife; pulverize. Add other ingredients and mix for 30 seconds. Pour into bottle and refrigerate. Allow liqueur to age at least one week before serving. The color will intensify as it ages, until it reaches the traditional shade of yellow. We find that this liqueur mellows to perfection 2 to 3 weeks after preparation.

VARIATION: For a different flavor, substitute from 1/4 to 3/4 cup French brandy for that portion of the vodka.

DUTCH CHOCOLATE-MINT LIQUEUR

Vandermint liqueur is a true Dutch treasure. Our recipe effectively simulates the richness of chocolate with a refreshing mint taste that made Vandermint famous. A perfect liqueur to serve in place of dessert. Makes about 1/2 pint.

1 cup Creme de Cacao Liqueur*
1/4 tsp. mint extract (spearmint, peppermint, or both)
1 Tbsp. brandy

Combine all ingredients in aging container. Cap and let stand 24 hours. Rebottle if desired. Serve.

*NOTE: Creme de Cacao Liqueur should be fully aged.

ENGLISH DAMSON PLUM LIQUEUR

No English kitchen would be without Damson plums. They are eaten fresh or put into jams, conserves and full-bodied English liqueurs. Your Damson Plum Liqueur is perfect in an authentic English Trifle.

2-1/2 lbs. Damson plums, washed, pitted and halved
2 cups granulated sugar
1 cup pure grain alcohol <u>and</u>
1 cup water
2/3 cup brandy

Place prepared plums in large aging container. Sprinkle sugar over plums and mix gently with a wooden spoon. Pour alcohol, water and brandy over mixture; stir gently. Cap and set in a cool dark place for 3 months. Stir or shake aging container weekly.

After initial aging, strain through colander into large bowl. With potato masher or back of wooden spoon, press juice from plums. Discard plums. Re-strain liqueur through fine cloth until desired clarity is reached. Place in aging container or bottles and age 1 additional month before serving.

France

CREME DE CACAO

Chocolate has been a favorite since the days of the Aztecs. One of the more exotic uses for chocolate is as a liqueur. The French Creme de Cacao Liqueur is perhaps the most famous.

Two of the problems with homemade chocolate liqueur have been the accumulation of sediment in the aging container and the resulting lack of true chocolate flavor. Our simple recipe solves both problems deliciously. It makes slightly less than one fifth.

1 cup granulated sugar
1/2 cup water
2 3-oz. packets unsweetened liquid chocolate
     (i.e., Choco-bake)
2 cups vodka
1 tsp. vanilla extract
1/2 tsp. glycerine

Combine sugar and water in small saucepan and heat until mixture comes to a boil. Reduce heat and stir constantly until sugar is completely dissolved. Set aside and let cool.

In aging container, combine chocolate, vodka and vanilla extract, stirring well to combine. Add cooled sugar syrup. Stir, cap and let age for one month in a cool dark place.

After initial aging, strain liqueur by placing a cloth bag inside a strainer set over a large bowl. Repeat as necessary for clarity. Add glycerine to strained liqueur. Bottle as desired and let age for an additional 2 months, minimum.

FRESH MINT LIQUEUR

In our search for natural-based liqueurs, we automatically turned to our home-grown mint beds to reproduce Creme de Menthe Liqueur. What we achieved was a fresher, milder, more delicate liqueur that is in many ways superior to the original. You may wish to try both recipes to discover your own preference.
Makes approximately 1 quart.

1-1/4 cups fresh mint leaves, slightly packed
3 cups vodka
2 cups granulated sugar
1 cup water
1 tsp. glycerine
8 drops green food coloring
2 drops blue food coloring

Wash leaves in cold water several times. Shake or pat dry gently. Snip each leaf in half or thirds; discard stems. Measure cut mint leaves, packing slightly.

Combine mint leaves and vodka in aging container. Cap and let stand in a cool place for 2 weeks, shaking occasionally.

After initial aging, pour liqueur through colander into a large bowl to remove leaves; discard leaves.

In saucepan, combine sugar and water. Bring to a boil, stirring constantly. Let cool. Add cooled sugar syrup to mint liqueur base, stirring to combine. Add glycerine and food color; pour into aging container for secondary aging of 1 to 3 more months.

VARIATION: Fresh Creme de Menthe: If you like a slightly heavier emphasis on the mint, adjust to taste by adding drops of mint extract (up to 1 tsp.) to the Fresh Mint Liqueur.

CREME DE MENTHE

This more traditional liqueur uses extract rather than fresh mint. It can be made in the three commercial shades of clear, gold and green. Makes approximately 1-1/4 quarts.

4 cups granulated sugar
2 cups water
3 cups vodka
1 Tbsp. mint or peppermint extract
1 tsp. glycerine

In saucepan, combine water and sugar. Bring to a boil, stirring constantly. When sugar is dissolved, set aside to cool.

In aging container, combine remaining ingredients. Add cooled sugar syrup, stirring to combine. Rebottle now or after initial 1 month aging.

VARIATIONS: Gold Creme de Menthe: Add yellow food coloring, a touch of red, and merest hint of blue, by drops, to the basic clear recipe until desired color is achieved. (We suggest that you practice with food coloring and water first!) Age as directed.

Green Creme de Menthe: Add green and blue food coloring, by drops, until desired color is reached. Age as directed.

GRAND ORANGE-COGNAC LIQUEUR

Grand Marnier is a classic orange liqueur to be savored. You will enjoy our Grand Orange-Cognac Liqueur just as much if you use a good French cognac to make it. This recipe makes about 1 pint.

1/3 cup orange zest*
1/2 cup sugar
2 cups cognac
1/2 tsp. glycerine

Place zest and sugar in a small bowl. Mash and mix together with the back of a wooden spoon or a pestle. Continue mashing until sugar is absorbed into the orange zest and is no longer distinct. Place into aging container. Add cognac. Stir, cap and let age in a cool dark place 2 to 3 months, shaking monthly.

After initial aging, pour through fine mesh strainer placed over medium bowl. Rinse out aging container. Pour glycerine into aging container. Place strainer on top of aging container and place cloth bag inside strainer. Pour liqueur back through cloth bag. Stir with a wooden spoon to combine. Cap and age 3 more months before serving.

*NOTE: Authentic Grand Marnier uses bitter Haitian oranges to produce its classic taste. You may use any type of orange peel you wish, however a bitter type, such as Seville, is preferred for authenticity.

CREME DE PRUNELLE

We set out to reproduce the French liqueur that is made from a variety of plum known as 'prunelle'. Our efforts were splendidly rewarded! While we anticipated that this would be a good liqueur, we were surprised that it turned out to be a <u>great</u> liqueur. Our Creme de Prunelle is what we would call a real 'sleeper'. It is perfectly wonderful in a wide variety of meat recipes, especially pork, and is a delight to sip.

1-1/2 lbs. dried pitted prunes
2 cups granulated sugar
2-1/4 cups vodka
1-1/2 cups brandy

Cut prunes into quarters; place in aging container. Add sugar, vodka and brandy; stir well to combine. Cap tightly and let age in a cool dark place for one month. Shake container every few days.

After aging, pour off liquid through a wire strainer into a large bowl. With a potato masher or the back of a wooden spoon, press the fruit to remove the remainder of the juice. Repeat straining process, using finer straining materials until desired clarity is reached. Bottle, seal and age an additional 2 to 4 months.

VARIATION: Spiced Creme de Prunelle is an American variation of this French favorite. Simply add a 3" cinnamon stick and 8 whole allspice to the initial ingredients. Let age as directed and remove spices at first straining.

 Germany

APPEL LIQUEUR

This wonderful apple liqueur will remind you of fall. It has been made in Germany since the 1700's and is called either 'appel liqueur' or 'appel schnaaps'. Traditionally it is unspiced but you may also enjoy our spicy cinnamon variation.

1-1/4 lbs. sweet apples
1 cup vodka
1 cup brandy
1 cup granulated sugar
1/2 cup water

Wash and de-stem apples; cut into wedges or slices. Put into aging container. Pour vodka and brandy over apples, stirring with a wooden spoon. Cap tightly and let age for 1 month.

Pour off liquid through a fine cloth bag into a large bowl; reserve apples. Pour strained liquid back into aging container. Place bag of apples in bowl. Twist to close bag top and press juice from apples with a potato masher or back of a wooden spoon. Pour released juice into aging container. Repeat process until all juice is removed. Half or more of your Appel Liqueur is locked inside the soaked, aging apples. Be sure to press out all the golden liquid.

Combine sugar and water in a small saucepan. Heat to a boil, stirring constantly. Set aside to cool. When cool, add to strained apple liquid in aging container. Cap and let age 1 to 2 months.

VARIATION: To make Spiced Appel Liqueur, add one 3" cinnamon stock and 5 cloves to the initial ingredients. Let age as directed but remove spices before pressing liquid from apples.

KUMMEL LIQUEUR

Caraway seeds, which are actually the dried fruit of the Carum Carvi plant, are the predominant flavoring in this Old World liqueur. The versatile Kummel will become a favorite before-dinner aperitif or an after-dinner refresher, as well as a unique ingredient in many drinks. Used in cooking, it will lace your breads, vegetables, sausages and pork dishes with its warm, aromatic goodness.
Makes just over 1 fifth.

2-1/2 Tbsp. caraway seeds
1/4 tsp. fennel seeds
2 whole cloves
3 cups vodka <u>or</u>
    1-1/2 cups pure grain alcohol <u>and</u>
    1-1/2 cups water
1/2 cup water
2/3 cup sugar

'Bruise' caraway and fennel seeds with pestle or the back of a wooden spoon. Place in aging container with whole cloves. Stir in alcohol base. Cap and let stand 24 hours. Remove cloves, recap and let age 2 to 3 more weeks in a cool, dark place. Shake occasionally.

After initial aging, strain off seeds. Combine sugar and water in a saucepan and heat to a boil, stirring to dissolve sugar. Remove from heat and let cool. Add cooled sugar syrup to liqueur; stir. Cap and age 1 to 2 months more.

Re-strain, if necessary, to make liqueur particle-free. Rebottle as desired.

OUZO

You need the strength of a Greek god to drink Ouzo. This liqueur is an anise-flavored test of manhood that will delight some and flatten others. Use sparingly in cooking for its unique anise flavor. Makes about 1 fifth.

1/2 cup boiling water
4 tsp. granulated sugar
1/4 tsp. angelica root, chopped
pinch of mace
4 tsp. anise extract
1-1/2 cups pure grain alcohol
3/4 to 1 cup water*

*You may adjust the alcohol strength to your taste (within the given range) and still have an authentic Ouzo.

Combine boiling water and sugar in the aging container; stir or shake until sugar is dissolved. Stir in angelica root and mace. Cool to lukewarm, then add anise extract, pure grain alcohol and water. Shake to combine.

Cover the let stand for 3 days. Strain and rebottle. Allow this liqueur to age for 1 month.

H & C's IRISH CREAM

In our testing for an Irish Cream liqueur, we used, as our standard, Bailey's Original Irish Cream... so good and so expensive! We found this one of the most difficult liqueurs to reproduce. We tried lots of 'homemade' recipes but all missed the mark of our standard: the best. So we threw everything out (except the Bailey's) and started again. Relax; we finally got it... so good and so inexpensive! Makes approximately 1 fifth.

2 eggs
2 small cans (5.33 oz. each) evaporated milk
1/2 tsp. chocolate syrup
1 Tbsp. vanilla extract
1/3 tsp. lemon extract
1/4 tsp. instant coffee
3/4 cup granulated sugar
1-3/4 cups Irish whiskey

Place all ingredients in blender; blend well. Bottle and let mellow in refrigerator at least one week before serving. We found this best after 2 to 4 weeks. Keep liqueur refrigerated.

 *Italy*

AMARETTO

While there are many Italian, French and American almond liqueurs on the market today, the oldest and best known is the original "Amaretto di Saronno" made in Italy since the fifteenth century. Because of its popularity and, in our opinion, premiere quality, we chose it as the standard for our testing comparisons. Tastes, however, will vary and for this reason we include a variation that will produce more of the 'bitter almond' flavor. This recipe makes slightly less than 1 fifth.

1 cup granulated sugar
3/4 cup water
2 dried apricot halves
1 Tbsp. almond extract
1/2 cup pure grain alcohol <u>and</u>
1/2 cup water
1 cup brandy
3 drops yellow food coloring
6 drops red food coloring
2 drops blue food coloring
1/2 tsp. glycerine, optional

Combine sugar and 3/4 cup water in small saucepan; bring to a boil, stirring constantly. Reduce heat and simmer until all sugar is dissolved. Remove from heat and cool.

In aging container, combine apricot halves, almond extract and alcohol with the 1/2 cup water and brandy. Stir in cooled sugar syrup mixture. Cap and let age 2 days. Remove apricot halves. (Save apricot halves, as they may be used in cooking.) Add food coloring and glycerine, if desired. Stir, recap and continue aging for 1 to 2 months.

Rebottle as desired. Liqueur is ready to serve but will continue to improve with additional aging.

VARIATION: For a more prominent 'bitter almond' flavor, add 4 apricot nuts*, split in half, to basic mixture. Leave in the liqueur 2 days to 2 weeks, depending upon the depth of flavor desired. Remove and discard apricot nuts. Continue as directed.

*NOTE: Apricot 'nuts' come from within the apricot pit. You may split apricot pits yourself or obtain them dried at a health food store.

ANISETTE

Italian Anisette is an anise-flavored liqueur that is sweeter and gentler than the Greek Ouzo. Delightful in our buttery ITALIAN ANISE STAR cookies. Makes about 1 quart.

1 tsp. coriander seed
5 tsp. anise extract
1 fifth vodka
2 cups light corn syrup

Crush coriander seeds in a mortar or small bowl, using pestle or back of spoon. Place in aging container. Add other ingredients to aging container. Cap and shake well to combine. Let stand in a cool dark place for one month, shaking every few days.

After initial aging, strain liqueur through fine cloth bag placed in wire mesh strainer, over a large bowl. Bottle and age an additional 2 months.

ITALIAN GOLD LIQUEUR

Liquore Galliano, that brilliant yellow liqueur in the tall, skinny bottle, is a popular challenge to the 'at-home' liqueur maker and is one of the most difficult to copy accurately. We tested countless recipes that didn't even come close to the original, before developing a quality liqueur of sufficient complexity that did.

Almost without exception, every homemade recipe we found used 80 proof vodka. However, in our search for authentic flavor, we found that a stronger alcohol base was mandatory. Therefore, we used pure grain alcohol and suggest that you follow our guidelines. 100 proof vodka, where available, would be an adequate substitute. This recipe makes approximately 1 quart.

1 tsp. chopped angelica root
1 3 inch stick cinnamon
1 whole clove
1 pinch nutmeg
1 vanilla bean, split
2-1/2 cups water*
2 cups sugar
1 Tbsp. lemon juice
1/2 tsp. anise extract
1/2 tsp. banana extract
scant 1/2 tsp. pineapple extract
1-1/2 cups pure grain alcohol*
1 tsp. glycerine
2 to 3 drops yellow food coloring

*If substituting 100 proof vodka for the alcohol, use 3 cups of vodka and reduce the water to 1 cup.

Line a wire mesh strainer with a paper coffee filter. Set strainer over a one quart mixing bowl.

Place angelica root, cinnamon, clove, nutmeg and vanilla bean in a medium saucepan. Add water; heat until mixture comes to a boil. Remove from heat. Let stand 15 seconds, then pour through the prepared strainer into the bowl. (It is important to work quickly or spices will impart too strong a color and taste to the liquid.) Reserve the vanilla bean; discard the other spices.

Rinse the saucepan and pour the liquid back into it. Add the reserved vanilla bean and the sugar. Heat until mixture comes to a boil; reduce heat and simmer 1 minute, stirring constantly. Remove from heat and cool to room temperature.

When cool, add the lemon juice, extracts, and alcohol, stirring to combine. Pour into aging container. Cap and let age in a cool dark place for 1 week.

After initial aging, strain through a cloth bag set in a wire mesh strainer over a large bowl. Repeat until desired clarity is reached. Stir in glycerine and food coloring. Bottle, seal and age for 3 to 6 months.

ITALIAN HAZELNUT LIQUEUR

Oregon hazelnuts are a key ingredient in this simulation of the delicate Italian Frangelico liqueur. Makes about 1 quart.

4 cups (approx. 1-1/8 lb.) unshelled hazelnuts (filberts)
1 fifth vodka
1 tsp. chopped angelica root
1/2 vanilla bean, split
1/4 tsp. almond extract
1-1/2 cups granulated sugar
1 cup water
1 tsp. glycerine
1 to 2 drops yellow food coloring (optional, to correct color if necessary)

Preheat oven to 350°F. Shell hazelnuts. Roast nuts by placing them on a baking sheet in the oven for 10 to 15 minutes. Remove from oven, coarsely chop hazelnuts and place in aging container. Stir in angelica root, vanilla bean, vodka and almond extract. Cap and let age for 1 month in a cool dark place, shaking occasionally.

After aging, pour through fine mesh strainer into a large bowl. Rinse out aging container. Place cloth bag or triple cheesecloth inside large funnel. Place funnel over aging container and pour liqueur through.

In medium saucepan, combine water and sugar; bring to a boil. Immediately reduce heat and simmer for a few minutes, stirring to dissolve sugar completely. Let cool. When sugar syrup has cooled, add to aging container, stirring well to combine. Cap and let age 3 months.

After second aging, re-strain through cloth or paper coffee filters until desired clarity is reached. Stir in glycerine and food coloring, if desired. Let age 2 more months before drinking.

SCOTTISH HIGHLAND LIQUEUR

The well-known and well-loved Drambuie is a Scottish tradition. As the legend is told, this herbal liqueur was once a favorite of Bonnie Prince Charlie who, in 1746, gave his secret recipe to the Mackinnons of Strathaird in gratitute for their shelter and assistance after his army was defeated.

The name Drambuie is derived from the Gaelic words 'an dram buidbeach' which mean 'the drink that satisfies'. That phrase applies as well to our Scottish Highland Liqueur. One sip and you're sure to hear the bagpipes! Makes 1 quart.

1 fifth Johnny Walker Black Label Scotch*
1-1/8 cups heather honey
2 tsp. angelica root, chopped
1/4 tsp. fennel seeds, crushed
2 2" strips lemon zest

Combine all ingredients in aging container. Cover tightly and shake gently several times during the first 24 hours. After 24 hours, remove the lemon zest. Cover again and let stand in a cool, dark place for 2 weeks, shaking gently every other day.

Strain through a wire sieve to remove the angelica root and fennel. Return to aging container, cover and let stand, undisturbed, in a cool, dark place for six months. Siphon clear liqueur into a sterile bottle, discarding the cloudy dregs.

*NOTE: We are very fussy about the scotch in this recipe!

CALIFORNIA LEMON LIQUEUR

We urge you to explore the many varied uses for this truly exquisite liqueur. Recipe makes approximately 1 fifth.

2 large lemons
2 cups granulated sugar
water (as needed)
2 cups vodka

Rinse lemons and pat dry. Thinly peel zest strips from lemons. Do not include white inner peel. Place zest strips into medium saucepan. Cut lemons in half and squeeze juice into measuring cup. Remove any seeds. Measure juice and add enough water to bring to the 1 cup mark. Pour lemon juice mixture into saucepan with zest, add sugar and stir. Bring mixture to a boil, stirring frequently. When it reaches a boil, reduce heat and simmer for 10 minutes. Remove from heat and cool.

Pour lemon mixture into aging container, add vodka and stir. Cap and age for 4 weeks in a cool dark place.

After initial aging, pour through metal strainer into bowl to remove zest. Pour back into aging container for an additional month of aging.

When the preliminary aging is completed, strain liqueur into large bowl by pouring through cloth bag which is placed in a strainer. Repeat straining until desired clarity is reached. Bottle and cap as desired. Liqueur is now ready to be used in cooking but for drinking, age 3 more months.

HAWAIIAN FRUIT LIQUEUR

The tropical islands of Hawaii boast huge pineapple plantations. Sweet, juicy pineapples blended with ripe bananas and laced with Hawaiian rum form the basis for this truly luscious liqueur. You will find it a versatile performer in many mixed drinks, punches and foods. Makes over 1 quart.

3 large bananas, peeled
2 cups canned pineapple chunks in unsweetened juice; drain and reserve juice
1 fifth light rum
1-1/4 cups granulated sugar
1 cup pineapple juice (reserved)
3" piece vanilla bean
6 drops yellow food coloring

Mash banana. Quickly combine banana, pineapple chunks and rum in an aging container.

In small saucepan, combine sugar, reserved juice and vanilla bean. Bring to a boil. Boil for 1 minute, stirring constantly. Cool to lukewarm. Add the sugar syrup to the fruit and rum mixture; stir to mix well. Cover and let stand in a cool, dark place for 1 month, stirring at least once a week.

After initial aging, strain through colander into a large bowl. Press fruit with potato masher or back of wooden spoon to obtain the juice. Discard the fruit and vanilla bean. Re-strain this liqueur several times, using progressively finer filtering material until maximum clarity is achieved. Return to aging container or bottle. Add 6 drops of yellow food coloring; mix well. Age for 1 month, minimum, before serving. If sediments form at bottom of bottle, re-strain and rebottle.

TABOO LIQUEUR

In writing this book, we have had to research, create, test, sample, rework, retest, sample, sample, sample. Even though the task has been difficult, we and our panel of tasters unanimously agreed that this liqueur was worth the entire effort of writing the book. In fact, our panel said, "Market it; it's that good". But rather than market this exquisite liqueur, so reminiscent of Forbidden Fruits, we offer it to you, our readers, with all good wishes and good cheer. Makes over 1 quart.

1 cup freshly squeezed grapefruit juice (approximately 2 grapefruits)
1 cup freshly squeezed orange juice (2 to 3 oranges)
1/4 cup freshly squeezed lemon juice (1 to 2 lemons)
shaved peel from 1 orange, chopped
shaved peel from 1 lemon, chopped
2-1/4 cups granulated sugar
4" piece of vanilla bean, split
1 cup brandy
1 cup vodka

In medium saucepan, combine grapefruit, orange and lemon juice, peel, sugar and vanilla bean. Bring to a boil. Reduce heat; simmer, stirring frequently for 10 to 12 minutes. Cool to lukewarm. Pour into aging container; add brandy and vodka. Allow liqueur to age for 3 weeks, then strain several times using successively finer strainers. For maximum clarity, let liqueur stand for several days between strainings. Pour liqueur into bottles and cap well.

VARIATION: You may choose to substitute honey for all or part of the sugar. Another variation for whiskey-lovers: try substituting American whiskey for the brandy.

MEXICAN COFFEE LIQUEUR

No book on liqueur making would be complete without a coffee liqueur recipe similar to Kahlua. In this case, research was no problem, since almost everyone who was aware of our project gave us their 'Kahlua-style' recipe. We really hoped one of them would be perfect, so we could move on to other liqueurs. However, this turned out to be one of the more difficult liqueurs to simulate.

There were three glaring errors in the majority of the 'homemade' liqueurs (and some of these are even in print!). First, true Kahlua is not just a simple mixture of instant coffee, sugar, water and vodka. Secondly, the brown sugar used in so many recipes produced a flavor completely foreign to the original. Thirdly, the alcohol base called for in many recipes, strangely enough, was the incorrect one or was vastly off in its proportions. It is important to bear in mind that this book of liqueur making is dedicated to producing the most accurate resemblence to the commercial counterpart. Makes approximately 1-1/2 quarts.

2 cups water
1/4 cup + 2 tsp. instant coffee granules or powder
3-1/2 cups granulated sugar
1 vanilla bean, split
2-3/4 cups vodka
3/4 cup brandy
1/4 tsp. chocolate extract
1 drop red food coloring

Heat water in medium saucepan. When hot, add coffee and stir until dissolved. Add sugar and vanilla bean, stirring well to combine. Bring to a boil, stirring constantly. Immediately reduce heat so that a very low boil is maintained for one minute. Remove from heat and cool to lukewarm.

Pour vodka and brandy into aging container. Add the cooled coffee mixture and the chocolate extract. Stir well. Cap and let age in a cool dark place for 3 weeks.

After initial aging, strain liqueur through a cloth-lined wire mesh strainer over a large bowl. Repeat until desired clarity is reached. Stir in food coloring. Bottle, cap and let age an additional 1 to 3 months.

Caribbean

NASSAU VANILLA LIQUEUR

This dark rum-based liqueur is similar to the well-known Nassau Royale. It may be served at room temperature or slightly warm, in the tradition of Amaretto Liqueur or a fine brandy. Our recipe makes just under a quart.

2-1/2 cups dark rum
4 vanilla beans, split in half
1 cup granulated sugar
1 cup water
1 tsp. glycerine (optional)

Combine rum and vanilla beans in aging container. Cap and shake to mix. Age in a cool dark place for 2 to 3 weeks.

In small saucepan combine sugar and water. Stir, over medium heat, until mixture comes to a boil. Remove from heat; continue stirring until all sugar is dissolved. Let cool.

Strain liqueur by pouring through coffee filter or cloth bag placed in strainer over medium bowl. Save vanilla beans.*

Combine cooled sugar syrup with liqueur. Stir in glycerine if desired. Bottle, cap and age an additional 1 to 2 months before serving.

MICROWAVE: Combine sugar and water in a 2-cup glass measure. Microwave on HIGH (100%) power for 30 seconds. Stir with wooden spoon. Microwave for 30 to 45 seconds more. Remove from microwave and stir until all sugar is dissolved. Let cool and proceed as directed.

*TIP: See page 88 for VANILLA SUGAR recipe. This is a great way to recycle those vanilla beans used for liqueur making.

PINA COLADA LIQUEUR

The Pina Colada cocktail has made this liqueur famous. Made with white Caribbean rum aged in oak casks, this original American liqueur will bring back memories of white beaches, crystal-clear waters and tropical sea breezes at a moment's notice. Makes approximately 1 quart.

1-1/2 cups granulated sugar
1-1/2 cups water
2 cups packaged flaked coconut
1 vanilla bean, split
24 chunks (approximately 1-1/4 cups) canned
    unsweetened pineapple, drained
3 cups light rum

Bring water and sugar to a boil. Reduce heat to low; add coconut and vanilla bean. Simmer 5 minutes, uncovered, stirring frequently. Remove from heat; add pineapple. Cool to lukewarm. Add rum. Place in aging container and let stand for one month, shaking once a week.

Pour through a fine wire mesh strainer into a large bowl. Press coconut and pineapple with potato masher or the back of a wooden spoon to obtain all the juice. Discard fruit. Strain liqueur through fine cloth or paper coffee filters several times until desired clarity is reached. Bottle and age an additional 1 to 2 months. If there is sediment at the bottom of the bottle, a final straining may be needed at this time.

Dutch West Indies

ORANGE CURACAO

Named after the Caribbean island of Curacao, this popular liqueur originated from Spanish citrus groves planted when the 'New World' was just opening. Today Curacao can be made with either the bitter or sweet orange varieties, as your taste dictates.

Curacao is traditionally clear or orange colored. More exotic are the dark orange, blue or green Curacao liqueurs. Our natural Orange Curacao is a cross between the clear and the orange color. By the simple addition of food coloring, you can make whatever shade you prefer. Makes approximately 1 fifth.

4 large oranges
1 tsp. whole coriander seeds
1 cup pure grain alcohol <u>and</u>
1 cup water
2 Tbsp. orange juice
2/3 cup granulated sugar
2/3 cup water

Place cake rack on cookie sheet. Turn oven on warm or lowest temperature.

Thinly peel the zest from oranges, using a swivel-bladed peeler or orange zester. Place on cake rack. Put into oven and leave until dry, about 1 hour. Let cool before continuing with recipe.

Crush coriander seeds coarsely with a pestle in a mortar bowl or with the back of a wooden spoon in a small bowl. Place seeds in aging container. Add dried zest, pure grain alcohol and the 1 cup water to the seeds.

Squeeze fresh oranges and measure 2 Tbsp. juice. Add to the aging container. Stir to combine. Cap and let age for 1-1/2 to 2 weeks, shaking once or twice.

After initial aging prepare sugar syrup. Combine sugar and 2/3 cup water in small saucepan. Bring to a boil, turn heat down and stir continuously until all sugar is dissolved. Remove from heat and let cool.

Strain orange mixture by pouring through cloth bag placed in a strainer over a large bowl. Rinse out aging container. Pour strained liqueur back into aging container. Add cooled sugar syrup to liqueur. Cap and let age in a cool dark place for 3 to 4 months.

OLD JAMAICAN COFFEE LIQUEUR

There are many well-known coffee liqueurs but one of the most popular is the Jamaican Tia Maria. Our rum-based recipe is similar to this famous liqueur.

Naturally, the taste will vary depending upon the types of rum and coffee used. For authenticity, use Jamaican light rum and a premium quality instant coffee. Makes approximately 1-1/2 quarts.

2-1/2 cups water
1/4 cup instant coffee granules or powder*
2 cups granulated sugar
1 vanilla bean, split
1 fifth light rum
1-1/2 tsp. glycerine

*A freshly opened jar of coffee will give the best results.

Heat water in a medium saucepan. When hot, stir in coffee until dissolved. Add sugar and vanilla bean, stirring to combine. Bring to a boil, lower heat and simmer for one minute, stirring constantly. Remove from heat; cool to lukewarm.

When cool, add rum; stir well. Pour into aging container, cover tightly and allow the liqueur to age 3 weeks in a cool dark place.

After initial aging, strain liqueur through a cloth-lined wire mesh strainer over a large bowl. Add glycerine, rebottle and age an additional 1 to 3 months.

Serving And Mixing Liqueurs

SERVING LIQUEURS

Traditionally, liqueurs are served at room temperature in small, stemmed liqueur glasses. Some liqueurs, such as Amaretto, can be served slightly warmed in a brandy snifter (small portions, please!). Liqueurs are commonly served with after-dinner coffee but you will find many other special times and ways to serve them.

LIQUEURS ON ICE

A light cocktail or summer cooler may be made very simply with a variety of liqueurs. Fill an old-fashioned glass with ice cubes. Pour liqueur of your choice over and serve.

LIQUEUR COFFEES

After-dinner coffees are easy to make when you have a selection of liqueurs on hand. Coffees served in this manner provide an elegant finish to a meal and are often substituted for dessert. If your liqueur dictates, you may wish to top your coffee with either sweetened whipped cream or WHIPPED LIQUEUR CREAM. These coffees may be served in either demitasse or coffee cups, mugs, footed coffee cups or glasses, depending upon the occasion.

While almost any liqueur works well with coffee, some of our favorites are: Amaretto, Creme de Menthe, Dutch Chocolate-Mint, Creme de Cacao, Danish Cherry, Irish Cream, Mexican Coffee, Old Jamaican Coffee, Orange Curacao and Scottish Highland. Recipe makes about 6 ounces, enough for 1 coffee or two demitasse cups.

5 oz. hot, freshly-brewed coffee
1/2 jigger (3/4 oz.) liqueur

Brew coffee to strength desired. Pour liqueur into coffee cup(s). Pour coffee over liqueur; stir to blend. Top with either sweetened whipped cream or WHIPPED LIQUEUR CREAM, if desired. Serve immediately.

LIQUEUR HOT CHOCOLATE

If you aren't a coffee lover, don't forget about hot chocolate. The addition of a small shot of a liqueur such as Irish Cream, Mexican Coffee, Danish Cherry, etc. can turn an old standard into a hot drink with real pizzaz.

LIQUEUR FRAPPE

For a simple but elegant drink, fill a stemmed glass with crushed ice. Pour 1-1/2 ounces of your favorite liqueur over and serve.

BITTER LEMON HIGHBALL

Pour 1-1/2 ounces of your favorite sweet liqueur into a highball glass. Add ice and fill with bitter lemon. Stir well.

FIZZES

Fizzes have the distinction of being a proper early or late morning beverage. Originally invented as a good tasting hangover panacea, they have become popular simply as an enjoyable drink. We suggest you try a FIZZ for festive late breakfasts, brunches or daytime parties.

A FIZZ is a light, fruity liquor drink, punctuated with the addition of carbonated (fizz) water. Usually seltzer or club sodas are used but experiment with any carbonated beverage if you like for a change of pace.

There are four basic types of fizzes:
- Plain Fizz: contains no egg
- Silver Fizz: egg white added
- Golden Fizz: egg yolk added
- Royal Fizz: whole egg added

BASIC FIZZ

2 oz. liqueur of your choice
1 tsp. superfine sugar*
juice of half a lemon or lime
club soda (or other carbonated beverage)

Pour all ingredients except soda into shaker can. Add 1 cup ice cubes, cover and shake. Strain into an 8-ounce highball glass. Fill with soda. Garnish as desired (with fruit, etc.) and serve.

NOTE: Egg Fizzes: we recommend using a blender rather than the shaker for this type. You may also wish to crack the ice or use 1/2 cup shaved ice.

*TIP: To make your own superfine sugar, see TIP on p. 76 (CHOCOLATE NUT RUFFLE).

ADULT MILKSHAKE

This liqueur 'milkshake' makes 1 serving. You may change the flavor of your milkshake by using any of the following liqueurs: California Lemon, Creme de Menthe, Creme de Cacao, Creme de Prunelle, Danish Cherry, Dutch Chocolate-Mint, English Damson Plum, Hawaiian Fruit, Italian Gold, Mexican Coffee, Old Jamaican Coffee, Orange Curacao, Pina Colada, or Taboo.

1/3 cup liqueur
1/4 cup crushed ice
1 scoop vanilla ice cream

Combine liqueur and ice in blender; process until well-blended. Add ice cream and blend just until combined.

Serve immediately in a chilled goblet and garnish as desired with fresh fruit, chocolate curls, maraschino cherry, etc.

ENGLISH HOT GROG

Makes two hearty mugs of grog. Ideal for sipping by the fire.

2 lemons
1 orange slice, cut in half
6 cloves
2 long cinnamon sticks
2 jiggers (1-1/2 oz. each) Nassau Vanilla
    Liqueur
boiling water

Wash lemons; cut in half. Place one slice of lemon and 1/2 slice of orange in each mug. Squeeze the juice from all remaining lemon halves and divide equally between the two mugs. Add 3 cloves, 1 cinnamon stick and 1 jigger liqueur to each mug. Fill with boiling water; stir with cinnamon stick. Serve hot.

HOT ELIZABETHAN POSSET

Taste a bit of history! This is a very old drink that has been popular since Elizabethan times. It was introduced to this country by Sir Walter Raleigh and was extremely popular in the South. Our Scottish Highland Liqueur lends a perfect flavor to this unusual drink. The recipe makes 6 servings.

4 eggs
1/4 cup granulated sugar
2 cups half-and-half
2 cups milk
1/3 cup granulated sugar
1 Tbsp. Amaretto Liqueur <u>or</u>
  1 tsp. almond extract
1 tsp. thinly shredded lemon rind
1 cup Scottish Highland Liqueur
6 tsp. toasted chopped almonds

Separate eggs, placing yolks in large and whites in small mixing bowl. Beat egg whites until frothy. Add 1/4 cup sugar slowly, beating constantly until stiff peaks are formed. Set aside. Beat egg yolks with electric or hand mixer until thick and lemon colored.

Heat milk, half-and-half and 1/3 cup sugar in a medium saucepan. Stir frequently and bring mixture to a low simmer. Slowly pour hot mixture into egg yolks, beating constantly. Beat in Amaretto <u>or</u> extract, Scottish Highland Liqueur and lemon.

Fold meringue into hot mixture and pour into 6 serving cups or mugs. Sprinkle 1 tsp. almonds on top of each drink. Serve immediately.

DUTCH 'ANIJS MELK'

In The Netherlands, where the winter sport of ice-skating on the canals is as popular today as it was hundreds of years ago, this drink is a popular 'warmer-upper'. We think it's perfect for after skiing, snowball fights or whatever cold winter sport you enjoy. It is traditionally served with cookies. Makes 4 to 5 servings.

4 cups whole or rich milk
1/4 cup Anisette Liqueur
1/3 cup sugar
2 Tbsp. cornstarch
2 to 3 Tbsp. water

Scald the milk in a medium saucepan; stir in sugar and simmer for 5 minutes. Dissolve the cornstarch in water and add to the milk mixture. Stir and cook over a low heat until the cornstarch is cooked, about 5 minutes. Remove from heat, stir in liqueur and pour into serving cups or mugs. Serve immediately.

AMERICAN WHISKEY PUNCH

Makes just over 1 gallon.

1 fifth whiskey
3 oz. Curacao Liqueur
6 oz. California Lemon Liqueur
4 cups orange juice
1 quart iced tea
1 quart club soda
1 lemon, sliced
1 lime, sliced
ice

Combine first 5 ingredients in punch bowl. Decorate with fruit. Add soda and ice before serving.

SANGRIA

Mix this in a large pitcher in front of your guests for party flair.

1-1/2 cups cracked ice
1/2 cup Orange Curacao Liqueur
1/2 cup California Lemon Liqueur
1 fifth red wine (Burgundy, red table wine
    preferred)
2 thinly sliced oranges
1 thinly sliced lemon
2 Tbsp. granulated sugar
1 to 2 cups club soda

Place ice in pitcher. Combine all ingredients.
Stir and serve.

THOR'S THUNDER PUNCH

This elegant punch is appropriate for any festive occasion. While this punch has 'punch', its fruity goodness will appeal to all. Makes 24 4-oz. servings.

1 large can (46 oz.) unsweetened pineapple juice
3-1/2 cups cherry juice from canned Bing or Royal Anne cherries, or any sweet cherry juice
2 cups orange juice
1/2 cup Orange Curacao or Grand Orange-Cognac Liqueur
1-1/2 cups Danish Cherry Liqueur
1/4 cup honey (orange blossom preferred)
1-1/2 cups brandy
2/3 cup lemon juice
2 quarts club soda or bitter lemon tonic
1 lime, thinly sliced

Chill all juices and soda or tonic for 24 hours.

When ready to serve, heat 1 cup of orange juice and the honey, stirring until honey is dissolved. Remove from heat and pour in remaining orange juice.

Pour pineapple and cherry juice into large punch bowl; add orange/honey mixture. Stir in remaining ingredients, except lime. Place lime slices on top of punch; add ice block float if desired.

Cooking With Liqueurs

Making your own liqueurs is just half the fun. The other half lies in using your liqueurs to add a gourmet touch to your special dishes. Even everyday fare can undergo a transformation with the addition of small amounts of liqueur. For example, baste your pork roast or pork chops with Creme de Prunelle before roasting or broiling and see what that little difference can do. When you are making gravy from the drippings, be sure to add a spoonful or two of Creme de Prunelle for flavor enhancement.

Baking opens up a whole realm of opportunities for using your homemade liqueurs. While most of the alcohol will evaporate if baked at higher temperatures, the essence of liqueur still adds flavor to the recipe. Many breads and muffins can be topped with a LIQUEUR GLAZE (see p. 63) which is not cooked and therefore keeps its full strength and flavor. Pie fillings offer the experimental cook a wide range of possibilities. One of our favorites is the addition of a couple of tablespoons of German Appel Liqueur to apple, raisin or mince pie fillings. Extraordinarily good!

It is no accident that liqueurs are added to the recipes in this book. In developing them, we set high standards. Each recipe and liqueur is a marriage of flavors; one would not be complete without the other. Some recipes are for homey meals, such as the NEWFIE GIRDLE CAKES WITH KUMMEL BUTTER. Others are 'impress-the-boss' specials, such as our DEVONSHIRE HAZELNUT ROLL or IRISH CREAM CUPS. Browse through the recipes and start with some of your favorites. We hope you'll try them all.

HINT O' MINT LAMB CHOPS AND STUFFING

The combination of lamb and mint is an international favorite. The English wouldn't think of serving lamb without mint sauce, while here in the United States, mint jelly with lamb has become a tradition. Whatever your preferences, we feel certain that our recipe will please the fussiest palate and create a new tradition of its own. This recipe serves 4 happy people!

8 rib lamb chops
1/3 cup chopped onion
1/2 cup finely chopped celery
1/3 cup minced, slightly packed, fresh mint leaves
1/4 cup butter or margarine
1 pkg. (6 oz.) dry herb-seasoned stuffing mix
1 beaten egg
dash of pepper
1/8 cup Creme de Menthe Liqueur
1 Tbsp. melted butter or margarine

Preheat oven to 350°F. Saute onion and celery in 1/4 cup butter until onion is translucent. Stir in mint leaves and stuffing mix. Remove from heat. Add pepper and beaten egg; stir well to combine. Place stuffing in a greased 3-quart baking dish.

Melt the 1 Tbsp. butter and let cool slightly. Add the liqueur to butter, stirring to combine. With pastry brush, cover both sides of lamb chops with butter/Creme de Menthe mixture. Arrange lamb chops on stuffing. Bake, uncovered, for 1 hour. Baste top of lamb chops again during the last 15 minutes of cooking time.

FRENCH COUNTRY PATE

An ideal recipe for entertaining because it is food processor easy and can be made ahead of time. The Creme de Prunelle adds mellowness to this mildly flavored pate.

2 medium onions
cooking oil
1 lb. fresh chicken livers, washed and patted dry
flour
seasoning salt and pepper, to taste
1 Tbsp. Creme de Prunelle

Peel onions and cut into fourths. Coursely chop onions in a food processor with a steel knife. Place a thin layer of oil in a large frying pan. Add onions and saute until medium brown in color. Remove onions from frying pan and set aside. Dip chicken livers into a mixture of flour, seasoning salt and pepper. Add additional oil to frying pan as necessary. Saute chicken livers over medium-low heat until no pink remains.

Place cooked chicken livers, onions, Creme de Prunelle and any cooking oil left in pan in the food processor work bowl. Process with steel knife until well blended, scraping down sides of bowl with a spatula as necessary. Spoon into serving container. Pat flat on the top. Cover with plastic wrap and refrigerate 8 hours or overnight before serving. Serve with SEASONED MELBA TOAST. Makes approximately 2 cups.

SEASONED MELBA TOAST

The perfect accompaniment to FRENCH COUNTRY PATE. This recipe makes a generous quantity that will warm a penny-pincher's heart.

1 long French bread or baguette
seasoning salt, to taste

Preheat oven to 350°F. With sharp knife, slice bread into 1/4" thick slices. Lay slices on cookie sheets, spacing so sides do not touch. Lightly sprinkle all slices with seasoning salt. Bake for 20 minutes, or until lightly browned and dry to the touch. Remove from oven and let stand at room temperature until cool and crisp. Place in dry plastic bags. Seal and set aside until needed. May be made up to 1 week prior to use. Keeps beautifully.

INTERNATIONAL CHEESE SOUP

As part of our cultural exchange program, we took gentle, mild-mannered Swiss cheese across the Alps to meet that flamboyant Greek, Ouzo. The partnership was dynamic, combining the best of both ethnic traditions in this hearty, yet subtly flavored soup. Our recipe makes 10 cups.

8 medium potatoes, peeled and diced
2 Tbsp. butter or margarine
2 medium onions, chopped
3 chicken broth cubes*, dissolved in
3 cups boiling water*
2 cups grated Swiss cheese
3 cups milk
1 Tbsp. Ouzo Liqueur
chopped chives or croutons, as garnish

Place potatoes in a large saucepan or soup pot. Cover with tap water and let stand 15 minutes.

In a medium skillet, melt butter or margarine. Add the onions and saute until limp and transparent. Remove from heat.

Drain potatoes into a colander, discarding the water. Return potatoes to the saucepan and add the boiling water containing the dissolved broth cubes. Bring to a boil, then lower heat and simmer, covered, until potatoes are soft. Remove from heat; stir in the onions. Cool to lukewarm.

Using a blender or food processor, puree 2 cups of the potato mixture at a time until creamy smooth. Repeat until all potato mixture has been processed. Place in large saucepan; add cheese and milk. Heat gently over medium-low heat, stirring constantly until cheese has melted and desired serving temperature is reached. (Do not allow soup to boil.) Just before serving, remove from heat and stir in the Ouzo. Garnish with croutons or chopped chives, if desired.

*NOTE: If you prefer to use homemade chicken broth, substitute 3 cups of broth for the broth cubes plus boiling water.

CALIFORNIA LEMON SAUCE

As bright and sunny as its name implies! You will find many uses for this versatile sauce.

3/4 cup water
1/2 cup granulated sugar
2 Tbsp. cornstarch
1 Tbsp. butter
1 egg, beaten
1/4 cup lemon juice
2 tsp. grated fresh lemon rind
2 Tbsp. California Lemon Liqueur

Bring water to a boil. In a small saucepan, combine sugar and cornstarch. Gradually stir in boiling water. Boil 1 minute, stirring constantly.

Remove from heat and stir in butter, lemon juice and rind. Gradually blend in egg and, finally, the liqueur. Serve slightly warm or cool over STEAMED ORANGE PUDDING, (see p. 87).

ORIENTAL PLUM SAUCE

Plum Sauce is the exotic cousin of Sweet-and-Sour sauce. Its rich, fruity taste combines plums and apricots with the added pizzaz of Grand Orange-Cognac Liqueur.

Serve this sauce with meats or poultry. It is especially good as a dipping sauce for egg rolls, fried won ton and Chinese chicken wings.

1/4 cup dried apricots
boiling water
1 cup fresh or frozen pitted red or purple plums*
2 Tbsp. water or plum juice*
1/2 cup granulated sugar*
1/2 tsp. dry powdered mustard
1/8 tsp. pepper
1/4 cup white vinegar
3 Tbsp. Grand Orange-Cognac Liqueur

Cover dried apricots with boiling water and let stand 10 minutes. Drain and finely chop apricots by hand or in a food processor with a steel knife/blade. Finely chop plums. Place fruit in a medium saucepan; add the 2 Tbsp. water or juice. Bring just to a boil, lower heat and simmer 15 minutes, stirring frequently. Add sugar, mustard and pepper. Simmer for 10 more minutes. Stir in vinegar. Simmer an additional 5 minutes. Remove from heat and cool to lukewarm. Stir in liqueur. Serve at room temperature or slightly warmed.

MICROWAVE: Prepare fruit as directed. Omit water from recipe. Place fruit in small mixing bowl and microwave on HIGH (100%) power for 2 minutes; stir. Reduce power to MEDIUM-LOW (50%) power and simmer for 5 minutes more. Stir every minute.

Add sugar and spices, mixing well. Simmer for 4 additional minutes on MEDIUM-LOW (50%) power, stirring after 2 minutes. Let cool and proceed as directed.

*NOTE: If you wish to use canned purple plums in this recipe, substitute 1 15-16 oz. can of drained and pitted plums for the fresh or frozen plums indicated. Decrease sugar to 1/4 cup; water or juice may not be necessary. The color will not be as ruby-rich but can be corrected by adding red food coloring. We do recommend that fresh or frozen plums be used where possible.

GOLDEN CREAM

True Galliano lovers will be delighted with any excuse to enjoy the flavor of their favorite liqueur. This recipe blends our Italian Gold Liqueur with fresh pineapple and creamed cheese for a unique topping or dip. Spoon over pound or tea cake, dip homemade doughnuts or beignets into it, or spread it on French toast, waffles or hot homemade bran muffins.

1 stick unsalted butter
1 pkg. (8 oz.) cream cheese
1 cup powdered sugar
2 Tbsp. Italian Gold Liqueur
3/4 cup fresh pineapple chunks*

*Fresh pineapple is preferred but pineapple canned in natural juice may be substituted. Drain well before use.

Cut butter and cream cheese into chunks. Place in food processor work bowl, fitted with steel knife/blade. Add powdered sugar and process until mixture is creamed. Add liqueur and pulse to combine. Add pineapple chunks and process by pulsing off and on until pineapple is in small chunks and mixture is well-combined.

MANDARIN YAM BAKE

Tired of the traditional marshmallow/sweet potato dishes? We are! This recipe is guaranteed not to have a marshmallow in it and is delightfully different and delicious. Try it at your next special meal. Serves 8.

5 cups (40-oz. can) canned yams or sweet potatoes, drained and mashed
1/4 cup melted butter or margarine
1/3 cup Taboo Liqueur
1 small can (11-oz.) drained mandarin oranges
1/4 cup chopped macadamia nuts, pecans or walnuts
1/3 cup firmly packed brown sugar
1 Tbsp. butter or margarine

Preheat oven to $375°$ F. Combine mashed yams, 1/4 cup melted butter and Taboo Liqueur in a 2 quart casserole dish; mix well. Gently fold in drained mandarin orange sections. Pat down evenly in casserole. Sprinkle brown sugar and nuts over top of casserole and dot with the 1 Tbsp. of butter. Bake for 30 minutes.

MICROWAVE: Cover dish with waxed paper. Cook on HIGH (100%) power for 7 to 8 minutes. Quarter turn dish halfway through cooking time, as necessary. Let rest 5 minutes for carry-over cooking before serving.

LIQUEUR GLAZE

Basic recipes with built-in variety are a real "find". Make this glaze with any liqueur and use it as a unique topping for baked goods.

1/2 cup confectioners' sugar
3-1/2 tsp. liqueur

In a small bowl, combine ingredients. Beat with whisk or beater until smooth.

NEWFIE GIRDLE CAKE WITH KUMMEL BUTTER

This title may require a little explanation! First, 'Newfie' refers to Canada's easternmost province, the island of Newfoundland. The Newfie style of cooking is warm and hearty, to offset the rigors of life on the stark, fog-bound coast.

The term 'girdle' has nothing to do with a woman's constricting garment but instead refers to the fact that the cake is baked on a griddle. In the evolution of language, the word 'griddle' has become 'girdle' in some dialects.

As in the world of Alice-in-Wonderland, where what is, isn't and what was, wasn't, so too our 'cake' isn't! Cake in this instance is actually a bread similar to a large scone or English muffin. This unique bread combines caraway seeds, molasses and currants, in the Newfie tradition. Topping it with Kummel flavored WHIPPED LIQUEUR BUTTER makes it a bread to remember. Serves 6-8.

3 cups flour
1/2 tsp. baking soda
1/4 tsp. salt
1 tsp. cream of tartar
2 Tbsp. granulated sugar
1/2 cup shortening
1 cup milk
2 Tbsp. molasses
3/4 cup dried currants or raisins
4 tsp. caraway seeds
WHIPPED LIQUEUR BUTTER made with Kummel Liqueur

Sift flour, baking soda, salt and cream of tartar together into a large mixing bowl. Stir in sugar. Cut in shortening until it resembles small peas. Add milk gradually, then molasses, mixing well to form a soft dough. Stir in currants and caraway seeds until well-combined.

Divide dough in half. On a lightly floured board, pat or roll out each half to a circle 3/8" thick. Cook on a lightly oiled griddle over low heat for 5 to 7 minutes. Turn over and cook the other side. (Slow cooking is essential so that the center of the bread will be thoroughly done, while the top and bottom are golden brown.)

Remove griddle from heat and let bread cool for 3 minutes. Brush top lightly with WHIPPED LIQUEUR BUTTER, made with Kummel Liqueur. Cut into wedges and serve warm with additional WHIPPED LIQUEUR BUTTER.

WHIPPED LIQUEUR BUTTER

1/4 lb. (1 stick) unsalted butter*
1 Tbsp. honey
1/4 tsp. grated fresh lemon peel (omit when using Kummel liqueur, as in recipe above)
1/4 cup liqueur

*Unsalted butter is preferred, but salted butter or margarine may be used.

Let butter reach room temperature. Combine all ingredients. Whip together until light and fluffy.

MICROWAVE: To soften refrigerator-cold butter quickly, unwrap cube and place in a microwave-safe bowl. Microwave on WARM (10%) power for 1-2 minutes. Let stand 2-3 minutes. Follow recipe directions as given.

GERMAN APPEL PANCAKE PUFF

This recipe is a cook's dream. It is quick and easy to prepare, economical, absolutely delicious, and a guaranteed 'showstopper'. Try it as an entree for your next special brunch, breakfast or late supper. Makes 3 to 4 servings.

3 apples, peeled and sliced
3 Tbsp. Appel Liqueur, spiced or unspiced
6 eggs, separated
1/4 cup all-purpose flour
1/4 cup melted butter or margarine
1/4 cup rich milk or half-and-half
2 Tbsp. butter or margarine

Topping:
4 Tbsp. sugar
1 tsp. ground cinnamon

Preheat oven to $400°$ F. Place peeled, sliced apples in medium mixing bowl. Pour liqueur over apples and stir gently to coat. Let stand while preparing pancake.

Beat egg yolks; mix in flour, melted butter and milk. Beat egg whites until they form stiff peaks. Fold beaten egg whites into flour mixture.

Heat 2 Tbsp. butter in a large skillet. When butter is melted, tilt pan to coat bottom and sides; pour in pancake batter. Spoon liqueured apples over top of batter to within 1/2" of edge.

Cook over medium heat for approximately 5 minutes. Transfer to oven and bake for 15 minutes or until golden brown. Top with cinnamon-sugar mixture, cut into wedges and serve hot.

ELEGANT CHOCOLATE CREPES

'Elegant' is the only word to describe this rich, French-inspired dessert. Serves 10 lucky people, 2 crepes each.

2 Tbsp. powdered cocoa (Dutch preferred)
1 cup sifted all-purpose flour
1/2 cup confectioners' sugar
4 eggs
1 cup milk
1/2 tsp. vanilla
2 Tbsp. melted butter or margarine
sweetened whipped cream
3/4 cup Creme de Cacao Liqueur

Sift the flour and cocoa into a medium mixing bowl. Stir in sugar and set aside.

Beat eggs until thick and lemon-colored. Stir in milk, vanilla and melted butter. Whisk egg mixture into flour mixture. Beat until a smooth batter is produced. Let batter stand 1 hour for more perfect crepes.

Heat a crepe or omelet pan over medium-low heat. Brush with cooking oil. Pour a small amount of batter into pan. Swirl pan so batter thinly coats the bottom. Cook until crepe is set and edges dry. Gently turn crepe over with spatula. Cook very briefly on second side. Remove crepe and repeat.

If serving immediately, place crepes directly onto serving plate(s), folding each into quarters. Hold in warming oven until all are prepared.

If making ahead (our favorite method), place crepe on lightly-oiled waxed paper (use a brush to oil the paper). Top with another piece of oiled waxed paper; repeat until all crepes are stacked. Wrap stack in aluminum foil and store in refrigerator or freezer until ready to use.

To reheat, loosen foil and place on a cookie sheet. Bake in a low oven, 275°F, until warm.

Whip cream and sweeten to taste. Place two crepes on each serving plate. Top with a generous dollop of whipped cream and drizzle 2 Tbsp. Creme de Cacao Liqueur over each serving. Serve immediately.

ALMOND TEA CAKE

This moist and perfectly yummy cake contains the wonderful ingredients that made Amaretto Liqueur famous: almonds and apricots. The liqueur itself adds a flavorful note to the cake and a richness to the special glaze. Just for fun, hide a whole almond in the batter before baking. The fortunate finder will have the best of luck for the next year!

Cake:
1 cup butter or margarine
1-1/3 cups granulated sugar
4 eggs
1/2 tsp. almond extract
1 cup lemon yogurt
2-1/2 cups all purpose flour
1 tsp. baking powder
1 tsp. baking soda
1 cup finely chopped, blanched almonds
1 whole shelled almond (optional)

Drizzle:
1 Tbsp. Amaretto Liqueur

Glaze and Decoration:
2/3 cup apricot jam
2 Tbsp. Amaretto Liqueur
3/4 cup finely chopped, blanched almonds
3/4 cup whole blanched almonds (optional)

Preheat oven to 350° F. Generously grease an 8" to 9" springform pan. Cut a circle of waxed paper to fit the bottom of the pan; place it in the pan and grease the paper. Flour the pan.

Cream butter or margarine. Add the sugar and cream well. Beat in 1 egg at a time, until all are combined. Stir in the almond extract and yogurt. Add the dry ingredients, beating well. Mix in the 1 cup chopped almonds. Pour into the prepared pan, press the whole almond into the batter (if desired) and bake for 50 to 60 minutes, until cake tester comes out clean.

Cool in pan for 10 minutes; remove sides of pan and cool to lukewarm. Pierce top of cake with a fork at 1" intervals, to a depth of 1/4". Drizzle liqueur over the surface of the cooled cake with a spoon.

Force apricot jam through a wire mesh strainer to obtain a smooth textured glaze. Add the 2 Tbsp. Amaretto, mixing well to combine. Spoon 3/4 of the glaze over the top and sides of the cake, covering the surface completely. Press the chopped almonds to the sides of the cake and decorate the top with whole almonds in a starburst pattern or a design of your choice. Spoon the remaining glaze over the top decoration.

VARIATION: For an ALMOND LAYER CAKE, increase the apricot jam to 1 cup and combine this with 2 Tbsp. + 2 tsp. Amaretto Liqueur, for the glaze. With a long knife, carefully split the cooled, undecorated cake into 2 layers. Drizzle each layer with 2 tsp. Amaretto. Spread a layer of the glaze over one layer of cake and top with the second cake layer. Glaze and decorate according to directions above.

APPLE PIE SNACK CAKE

The heady aroma of fall apples and warm spices fills the air as this moist cake bakes. A good 'anytime' treat.

Dry ingredients:
1-3/4 cups granulated sugar
2-1/2 cups cake flour
1/2 cup golden seedless raisins
1 tsp. ground cinnamon
1/4 tsp. ground cloves
1/2 tsp. ground allspice
1-1/2 tsp. baking soda
1/2 tsp. baking powder
1/2 tsp. salt (optional)
1/8 tsp. instant coffee

Liquid ingredients:
1/2 cup Spiced Appel Liqueur <u>or</u> Appel Liqueur
2 eggs
2/3 cup cooking oil
2 cups apple pie filling (home-canned is best)

Grease and flour 2 round cake pans or 2 9" square cake pans. Preheat oven to 350°F.

Combine all dry ingredients in a large mixing bowl; mix well.

In medium mixing bowl, beat eggs. Add rest of liquid ingredients; stir well until combined. Pour liquid ingredients into dry. Beat well to completely mix, scraping sides occasionally. Pour into prepared pans. Bake for 50 to 55 minutes. Test with toothpick for doneness. Cool on cake racks. Sprinkle with VANILLA SUGAR*, <u>or</u> place paper doily on top of cake and sift powdered sugar over to form design. Remove doily and serve slightly warm or at room temperature.

TIP: The second cake may be covered and frozen for later use. Bring to room temperature before serving.

*See page 88 for VANILLA SUGAR.

DEVONSHIRE HAZELNUT ROLL

Our tasters used such words as 'delicate', 'elegant' and 'exquisitely gourmet' to describe this subtly-flavored dessert. We couldn't have said it better! A light-as-air sponge cake is filled with our fluffy Devonshire cream, Oregon hazelnuts, chopped chocolate and, of course, our Italian Hazelnut Liqueur to create a perfect finale to a gourmet dinner. Serves 8.

Filling:
1 3-oz. package softened cream cheese
2 Tbsp. confectioners' sugar
2 Tbsp. Italian Hazelnut Liqueur
1 cup whipping cream
1/4 cup blanched hazelnuts
1/2 cup semi-sweet or milk chocolate candy

Sponge Cake:
cooking oil
1/2 cup superfine granulated sugar*
3 eggs
3/4 cup sifted cake flour

Drizzle:
1 Tbsp. Italian Hazelnut Liqueur
2 tsp. Italian Hazelnut Liqueur

Garnish:
confectioners' sugar
1 oz. semi-sweet chocolate, melted
whole blanched hazelnuts
chocolate leaves (optional) see p. 78

Prepare filling before making cake. Combine cream cheese, sugar and liqueur in a small bowl; set aside. Whip cream until soft peaks form. Add the cream cheese mixture, beating until stiff peaks form.

Insert steel knife/blade into food processor. Add whole hazelnuts and broken chunks or pieces of chocolate candy. Process by pulsing off and on until mixture is coarsely chopped. Fold gently into cream mixture. Chill until needed.

Move an oven shelf so that it is one notch above center. Preheat oven to 425° F. Line bottom of a 9-1/2" x 14" jelly roll pan with waxed paper. Brush paper and sides of pan with oil.

Place sugar in a pie plate and heat in oven for 4 minutes. (Sugar should be very hot but not melted.) While sugar is in oven, place eggs in a large mixing bowl and flour in a small bowl.

When sugar is hot, pour it immediately into the large bowl with the eggs, while beating at medium speed with an electric mixer. Continue beating for 7 minutes.

Remove beater. Sprinkle all of the flour over the surface of the batter. Fold the flour gently into the batter using a rubber spatula until all flour disappears. Spread batter evenly in prepared pan. Be sure corners are filled. Bake for 9 minutes or until golden. Remove from oven and turn out onto a baking sheet covered first with a clean towel, then with a large sheet of waxed paper. Roll cake, towel and paper together, jelly roll fashion, starting at the short end. Allow cake to cool to lukewarm while rolled.

When cool, unroll cake, sprinkle the 1 Tbsp. liqueur over the surface and spread filling evenly over top. Roll the cake and filling slowly. Place roll so that the visible edge is hidden below; drizzle the remaining 2 tsp. of liqueur over the top of the cake. Sprinkle with sifted confectioners' sugar. Dip half of each whole hazelnut in melted chocolate; cool. Garnish cake roll with a row or clusters of dipped nuts and chocolate leaves, if desired.

*TIP: To make your own superfine sugar, see TIP on p.75 . (CHOCOLATE NUT RUFFLE)

TRISTY'S TERRIFIC 'TRIFFLE'

We were going to name this recipe 'English Trifle'. However, when Heather's daughter Tristy first tasted this dessert, she exclaimed "what a terrific 'triffle'!" Hence, its new name, much more creative than our own.

If you enjoy a traditional trifle, you will find our liqueured version simply 'terriflic'! Makes 1 trifle, to serve 8-10.

Base:
1 standard size loaf pound cake <u>or</u>
1 9-1/2" x 14" sponge cake*
1 small jar (12-oz.) apricot preserves
4 tsp. sherry
1/2 cup English Damson Plum Liqueur

Custard:
1 envelope (3 Tbsp.) Birds English Custard
    (Dessert Mix)
3 Tbsp. granulated sugar
2 cups milk

Whipped Cream Topping:
1/2 pint whipping cream
2 Tbsp. granulated sugar
1/4 tsp. vanilla

Garnish:
1 tsp. unsalted butter or margarine
2 Tbsp. blanched, slivered almonds
1 whole red maraschino cherry

Cut pound or sponge cake into 3/4" wide slices or strips. Cut again to make each piece about 2" long. Place one layer of cake pieces in the bottom of a 1-1/2 to 2-quart glass bowl. Sprinkle 2 tsp. sherry and half the liqueur over cake. Spoon half the apricot jam over all.

Prepare custard as package directs, using milk and 3 Tbsp. sugar. Pour half of the hot custard over bottom layer.

Repeat with second layer. Cover with plastic wrap and refrigerate.

Place almonds and butter in small saucepan. Cook over medium heat, stirring constantly until almonds are lightly toasted. Remove from heat and let cool.

Whip cream until soft peaks form. Mix in vanilla and 2 Tbsp. sugar.

Spoon sweetened whipped cream over top of trifle. Place cherry in the center and ring with cooled slivered almonds. Chill for 2 hours before serving.

MICROWAVE:
Custard: Place Birds custard powder and sugar in medium sized, microwave safe mixing bowl. Pour cold milk into a 4-cup glass measure. Microwave on HIGH (100%) power for 2 minutes to heat. Pour heated milk into dry mixture, whisking well to mix.

Remove whisk and microwave on HIGH (100%) power for 2 minutes. Whisk well and continue for 1-1/2 minutes more. Whisk again.

Toasted almonds: Place almonds and butter in small glass custard cup or glass measure. Microwave for 1-1/2 to 2 minutes on HIGH (100%) power, stirring every 30 seconds, until almonds are lightly toasted. Let cool.

*NOTE: See page 71 for basic sponge cake recipe. Make as directed but do not roll up or drizzle with liqueur.

CHOCOLATE NUT RUFFLE

Try this for your next very special dessert. We guarantee it is 'decadence plus'! Serve in pretty demitasse cups or smaller footed glasses. Makes 8 demitasse servings.

1 cup superfine sugar**
3/4 cup cocoa powder (fine Dutch cocoa is preferred)
1/2 cup Old Jamaican Coffee Liqueur
4 egg yolks
1 cup whipping cream
1/2 cup chopped almonds, toasted
3/4 cup coarsely chopped semi-sweet chocolate
8 chocolate covered cherry cordial candies*
semi-sweet chocolate shavings for garnish

In the top portion of a double boiler, combine the sugar, cocoa and liqueur. Cook over medium heat 15 minutes, stirring constantly.

In a large bowl, beat the egg yolks with an electric mixer until slightly fluffy (1 to 2 minutes). With the mixer at medium speed, very slowly drizzle the hot chocolate mixture into the beaten yolks. Continue beating for 2 more minutes, scraping sides of bowl. Refrigerate until cold (30 to 45 minutes).

In medium bowl, whip cream until stiff peaks form. Add a spoonful of whipped cream to the chocolate and mix thoroughly to soften the chocolate. Fold in the remainder of the whipped cream, very gently. Add almonds and chopped chocolate, stirring just enough to combine them; be careful not to disturb the fluffiness of the whipped cream.

Fill 8 demitasse cups 1/3 full of chocolate mixture; place 1 candy in center of each. Spoon in more of the chocolate mixture until cups are 3/4 full and candy is hidden. Garnish with chocolate shavings and cover with plastic wrap. Place cups in freezer for at least 2 hours; serve frozen.

*VARIATION: To make an even more spectacular dessert, with food syringe and needle (available at gourmet food shops), extract cherry cordial liquid from the bottom of the candy. Replace with your homemade Old Jamaican Coffee Liqueur.

**TIP: To make your own superfine sugar, grind granulated sugar in your blender or food processor.

DUTCH LAWYERS' PIE

The verdict is in! The jury has decided that our DUTCH LAWYERS' PIE is a perfectly superb chiffon dessert. As proof, the jury was shown evidence of the pie's creamy Advocaat filling, unique coconut crust and surprise center layer. It was a decisive victory for the fans of good food everywhere.

1/4 cup melted butter or margarine
2-2/3 cups flaked coconut
1/2 cup granulated sugar
1 envelope (1 Tbsp.) unflavored gelatin
3 eggs, separated
3/4 cup milk
1/2 cup Advocaat Liqueur
1 cup whipping cream
1 tsp. vanilla extract
1/2 tsp. lemon extract
whipped cream for garnish, if desired

Preheat oven to 325°F.
In medium saucepan, melt butter or margarine; stir in flaked coconut. Press half of this mixture over bottom and sides of a 9-inch pie plate. Spread remainder on a baking sheet. Bake both for 10 to 15 minutes, or until coconut is golden brown. (Watch closely! The coconut on the baking sheet may cook more quickly than the crust.) Remove from oven and let cool.

In medium saucepan, combine 1/4 cup of the sugar, the gelatin, egg yolks and milk. Cook over medium-low heat, stirring constantly, until gelatin and sugar are completely dissolved. Cool to lukewarm; stir in the liqueur. Refrigerate until mixture is thick but not set.

In small mixing bowl, beat egg whites until soft peaks form. Add the remaining sugar gradually, while beating until stiff peaks form. Set aside.

In another small mixing bowl, whip the cream until stiff, gradually adding the vanilla and lemon extracts. Fold the cream gently into the gelatin mixture, then fold in the egg whites. (Be careful not to deflate them.) Refrigerate until mixture holds its shape when mounded.

Spoon half the filling mixture into the cooled crust. Cover with a layer of the toasted coconut, reserving 1/4 cup for garnish. Top with remaining filling. Chill until set. Garnish with additional whipped cream, if desired, and the reserved coconut.

IRISH CREAM CUPS

This dessert was designed for Irish Cream and chocolate lovers, which we figured must include just about everybody! Light, delicate Irish Cream filling nestles in each pretty chocolate cup and is topped with a party special garnish of whipped cream 'flowers' and chocolate 'leaves'. Try it...devastating! Makes 9 filled chocolate cups or filling will make one 9" pie.

Chocolate Cups:
1 bar (8 oz.) semi-sweet or milk chocolate candy
1/4 cup unsalted butter or margarine

Chocolate Leaves:
4 oz. semi-sweet or milk chocolate candy
2 Tbsp. unsalted butter or margarine
18 small leaves with prominent veins on back*

Irish Cream Filling:
3 Tbsp. cold water
1-1/2 tsp. gelatin
3 eggs, separated
3 Tbsp. granulated sugar
6 Tbsp. Irish Cream Liquer
3/4 cup sweetened whipped cream
additional sweetened whipped cream for garnish

 *Use either real, NONPOISONOUS leaves, washed and dried, or silk, foil or paper leaves available in cake decorating shops. Be sure the veins are prominent.

To prepare the chocolate cups, break chocolate into pieces and place in small saucepan. Add butter. Melt over low heat, stirring until mixture is smooth. Line 9 muffin cups with paper liners. Divide chocolate mixture evenly over bottom and up sides of paper liners, using the back of a spoon. Refrigerate to set.

MICROWAVE: Break chocolate pieces into a 2 cup glass measure. Add butter. Microwave on HIGH (100%) power, uncovered, for 45 seconds. Stir and microwave 35 to 45 seconds more. Stir again until smooth and completely melted. Do not overcook. Proceed as directed.

To make the chocolate leaves, prepare the melted chocolate and butter mixture according to directions above. (If using microwave, reduce each cooking time to 30 seconds.) With a small clean paintbrush, coat the back of each leaf with the melted chocolate mixture.

Cool to set and repeat with additional layers of chocolate for sturdiness. Set leaves on waxed paper covered baking sheet. Refrigerate until firm. Gently peel leaf away from chocolate. Refrigerate until needed.

Prepare filling. Put water in a small glass bowl or cup. Sprinkle gelatin over water and let stand for 5 minutes until spongy.

In medium bowl, whip egg whites until fluffy; add egg yolks, sugar and Irish Cream. Beat well for several minutes.

Place cup/bowl of gelatin in a small saucepan of hot water. Turn heat on low. When gelatin is dissolved, pour into egg mixture, beating well. Fold in sweetened whipped cream. Pour into prepared chocolate cups or pie shell (see variation). Refrigerate. When well chilled, paper may be carefully peeled away from the chocolate cups. Garnish just before serving with a small dollop of whipped cream (the 'flower') and two chocolate leaves. (Or simply top with whipped cream and shaved chocolate.)

VARIATION: Pour filling into CHOCOLATE-LOVERS' COOKIE PIE CRUST (see p. 80). Refrigerate. Top with additional whipped cream and garnish with chocolate leaves or shaved chocolate.

CHOCOLATE-LOVERS' COOKIE PIECRUST

You will find many uses for this wonderfully easy-to-make crust.

20 chocolate cream-filled sandwich cookies
3 Tbsp. melted butter or margarine
1 Tbsp. Dutch Chocolate-Mint Liqueur

Preheat oven to 350°F. Crush cookies by hand or in a food processor with a steel knife until finely crushed. (If using a food processor, turn it on while empty, then drop one cookie at a time through the feed tube.)

Pour cookie crumbs into a 9" pie plate; drizzle melted butter over it. Stir well to combine. Pat evenly to cover bottom and sides of pie plate. Bake for 10 to 12 minutes. Let cool slightly; drizzle liqueur over crust. Fill or refrigerate until ready to use.

MICROWAVE: Cook crust on HIGH (100% power) for 2 to 2-1/2 minutes, quarter turning halfway through cooking time. Proceed as directed.

ICE CREAM SOCIAL PIE

This pie has a rich, old-fashioned taste and is 'pretty as a picture'. It is easy to make and freezes beautifully for 'make-ahead' entertaining.

Fill CHOCOLATE-LOVERS' COOKIE PIECRUST with:
1-1/2 quarts French Vanilla <u>or</u> Chocolate Chip
    ice cream

Place ice cream in scoops, slightly mounding up in center. Set in freezer while making FUDGE SAUCE.

FUDGE SAUCE

4 pkgs. (1 oz. each) semi-sweet chocolate
1/3 cup sugar
2 Tbsp. butter or margarine
1/4 cup water
2 Tbsp. Dutch Chocolate-Mint Liqueur

You may crush the chocolate by hand and cook the sauce on top of the stove but the easiest method is to make it in your food processor.

Insert steel knife/blade in food processor. Break chocolate blocks into smaller pieces. Turn processor 'On' and drop pieces, one at a time, through feed tube. Process until finely minced.

Heat water and butter; stir in sugar. When sugar has dissolved, remove from heat and pour through feed tube with motor running. Last, add liqueur.

Pour sauce over frozen ice cream pie. Replace in freezer* while making WHIPPED LIQUEUR CREAM with either Creme de Menthe Liqueur or Fresh Mint Liqueur. Spread or pipe WHIPPED LIQUEUR CREAM over well-chilled pie. Optional: top with green maraschino cherry and/or chopped nuts.

*NOTE: If you wish to freeze pie ahead, cover with plastic wrap or aluminum foil as soon as fudge sauce has firmed in freezer. Add WHIPPED LIQUEUR CREAM just before serving.

TIP: Make gourmet hot fudge sundaes in a variety of flavors by changing the liqueur used in this recipe. We suggest Amaretto or Mexican Coffee Liqueur as a good beginning.

TROPICALE YOGURT PIE WITH GREEN 'BUTTERFLIES'

If you have been to Cabo San Lucas and gazed over the miles of white sands and clear blue seas, you may recall the shocks of fuschia bougainvillaeas with brilliant green butterflies amoung them. This pie brings back memories of the gentle tropical breezes that cool the Baja sun.

Make this recipe with any of our 'tropical' liqueurs and top with kiwi green butterflies. Especially good in warm weather. Recipe makes 1 pie.

1 baked graham cracker crust
1 envelope unflavored gelatin
2 Tbsp. boiling water
1 carton (8 oz.) unflavored yogurt
1/2 cup liqueur: either Pina Colada, Taboo, Orange Curacao, California Lemon or Hawaiian Fruit
1/3 cup granulated sugar
1 pint whipping cream
2-3 Tbsp. granulated sugar
1/2 tsp. vanilla extract
1 kiwi fruit
1 Tbsp. same liqueur as above

Peel and slice kiwi fruit into 8 slices. Cut each slice in half. Place slices in small bowl and drizzle 1 Tbsp. liqueur over. Set aside.

In a medium bowl, mix gelatin and 1/3 cup sugar. Add boiling water and stir or whisk until gelatin is completely dissolved. Whisk in yogurt and 1/2 cup liqueur until well combined. Refrigerate.

Beat whipping cream until soft peaks form. Remove half of whipping cream and fold into refrigerated mixture. Pour into prepared graham cracker crust.

Into remaining whipped cream, stir the 2-3 Tbsp. granulated sugar (to taste) and vanilla extract. Place 8 mounds of whipped cream around outer edge of pie. Stand 2 slices of kiwi into each whipped cream mound to form butterfly 'wings'.

WHIPPED LIQUEUR CREAM

1/2 pint whipping cream
2-3 Tbsp. confectioners' sugar
1 Tbsp. liqueur of your choice

Whip cream until soft peaks form. Add sugar; whip a bit more. Add liqueur and whip lightly to combine. Serve or chill, covered, until needed.

MOCHA TRUFFLES

Truffles! The name implies luxury, elegance and pure culinary delight. Our MOCHA TRUFFLES, with their combination of rich chocolate and Mexican Coffee Liqueur, easily live up to this romantic reputation. The recipe makes 3 to 3-1/2 dozen delectable confections.

12 oz. semi-sweet chocolate chips
4 Tbsp. (1/2 stick) butter or margarine
1/4 cup superfine granulated sugar
2 egg yolks, beaten
1 cup finely chopped blanched almonds
1/3 cup Mexican Coffee Liqueur
chocolate decorettes or pre-sweetened powdered
    cocoa mix*

Heat water in the bottom part of a double boiler. Place chocolate chips in the top half of the double boiler and stir until melted. Gradually stir in the butter or margarine. Add the sugar and continue to cook, stirring constantly until sugar is dissolved. Remove from heat and allow to cool as much as possible without letting chocolate harden. Quickly stir in the beaten egg yolks. Add the chopped almonds and mix well. Stir in the Mexican Coffee Liqueur. Refrigerate 15 minutes or until mixture is easily handled and not sticky.

Spread a layer of decorettes or powdered cocoa mix in a small bowl. With your hands, shape refrigerated mixture into small (3/4") balls. Roll in decorettes or cocoa mix to coat lightly. Chill until very firm.

*NOTE: Chocolate truffles are customarily coated with a fine dusting of unsweetened cocoa powder. However, in this recipe, we felt that the unsweetened chocolate overshadowed the delicate coffee liqueur flavor. Therefore, we have substituted a sweeter coating.

ITALIAN ANISE STARS

These tiny, buttery, melt-in-your-mouth stars have just the merest tantalizing hint of Anisette. Makes 9 dozen tiny stars.

1 cup butter
1/3 cup golden brown sugar
2-1/4 cups all-purpose flour
2 Tbsp. Anisette Liqueur

Preheat oven to 325°F. In a mixing bowl, cream the butter; add the sugar gradually, combining thoroughly. Mix in half of the flour until dough is smooth, then add the liqueur, beating until well blended.

Sprinkle the remaining flour over a pastry cloth or smooth rolling surface. Knead the dough on the floured surface until the excess flour has been worked into the dough. Refrigerate dough at least 1 hour for easier handling.

On a lightly floured surface, roll dough to 1/4" thickness. Use a 1-3/4" cookie cutter dipped in flour to cut the tiny star-shaped cookies. Transfer with a knife to an ungreased baking sheet; bake for 12 minutes or until just the edges are a light golden brown.

VARIATION: For a moist cookie with a more pronounced anise flavor, brush the tops of the stars while still hot, with a glaze made from one tsp. granulated sugar combined with 2 tsp. Anisette Liqueur.

DANISH FRUIT SOUP

Winter fruits are the stars of this nontraditional 'soup'. It is to be served for a gourmet brunch or as a special Scandinavian dessert. When served as a dessert, you may wish to top it with sweetened whipped cream, sour cream or WHIPPED LIQUEUR CREAM (see p. 83). Recipe serves 12 generously.

2-1/2 cups water*
1/2 cup pitted prunes
1/2 cup raisins
1/2 cup dried pitted cherries <u>or</u>
    1 cup canned pitted cherries*
2 apples, peeled, cored and sliced
1 orange, peeled and sliced <u>or</u>
    1 small can (11 oz.) mandarin orange sections*
3/4 cup granulated sugar
1/4 cup tapioca
1 stick cinnamon
2 cups white grape juice <u>or</u>
    apple juice
1/2 cup Danish Cherry Liqueur

*If using either of the canned orange or cherry options, be sure to drain juice and reserve. Measure juice as a part of the water measurement.

In a large saucepan, combine water, prunes, raisins, and dried cherries (if used). Bring to a boil. Stir and reduce heat to a low simmer. Cover and simmer for 10 minutes.

Add all remaining fruits, sugar, tapioca, cinnamon and half the grape or apple juice. Simmer for 15 minutes, stirring occasionally until slightly thickened. Stir in remaining juice and let cool. When cool, stir in Danish Cherry Liqueur. Refrigerate. Serve well chilled.

STEAMED ORANGE PUDDING

Moist, cake-like steamed puddings have long been an English and Canadian favorite. With our easy 'oven-steaming' method, you can prepare this warm and homey dessert in less than half the time of stove-top steaming. Serve slightly warm, with or without a custard or CALIFORNIA LEMON SAUCE, (see p. 60).

1/2 cup sultana raisins
1/4 cup dark raisins
1/4 cup Curacao Liqueur
1 cup dry breadcrumbs
3/4 cup all-purpose flour
1/3 cup brown sugar
1/2 cup granulated sugar
1 tsp. baking soda
1/4 cup scalded milk
1/4 cup cold milk
1 beaten egg
1/2 cup or 1 stick butter or margarine, melted
1 tsp. freshly grated orange peel
1/2 tsp. freshly grated lemon peel
2 to 3 Tbsp. Curacao Liqueur

Preheat oven to 375°F. Measure raisins; pour the 1/4 cup liqueur over them. Let stand until needed.

Mix bread crumbs, flour, sugars, orange and lemon peels in food processor (or mixing bowl). Pulse (or stir) until well mixed.

Stir the baking soda into the scalded milk, then add remaining milk. Pour milk mixture into mixing bowl; add beaten egg and melted butter. Combine with flour mixture; beat well. Stir in the raisin/liqueur mixture.

Spoon batter into well-buttered 1-quart baking dish. Cover top with aluminum foil, sealing down all around. Pour about 3/4" to 1" of water into a cake pan; place the 1-quart baking dish inside it. Set these carefully into the oven. Bake 1-1/4 hours. Test center with toothpick; pudding should be moist but toothpick will remain clean when tested.

Spoon the 2 to 3 Tbsp. liqueur over the warm pudding. Let cool slightly before slicing or spooning out servings.

VANILLA SUGAR

This is excellent for desserts and confections and is a good way to make full use of the vanilla beans used in liqueur making.

Rinse vanilla beans in cool water. Place on a doubled paper towel and pat tops dry with another paper towel. Let dry completely.

When dry, place in a pint jar and add two cups granulated sugar. Let age at least a few days before using.

HIGHLAND MARMALADE

Put some of our Highland Marmalade on a hot breakfast scone. Take a bite, close your eyes and you will almost feel the Scottish mist curl at your feet, with the smell of the heather in bloom surrounding you. Top a jar with a piece of tartan fabric for the perfect gift to any Scotsman or lover of Scotch. This recipe fills 7 6-oz. jelly jars.

4 large, sweet oranges (Valencia or other sweet variety)
1 medium lemon
8 cups water
8 cups granulated sugar
2-3/4 cups water
1/2 cup Scottish Highland Liqueur

Wash oranges and lemon. Trim ends and cut into quarters. Remove and discard all seeds. Thinly shred oranges and lemon by hand or with shredding disc of food processor. Pour shredded fruit and accumulated juice into large glass or ceramic bowl(s); add the 8 cups of water. Cover with plastic wrap and let stand 24 hours.

Remove any large pieces of improperly cut rind and fruit membrane; discard. Pour shredded fruit and juice into an 8-quart or larger saucepan or canning kettle. Add remaining 2-3/4 cups water and bring mixture to a boil. Turn heat down so that a low boil is maintained. Stir in sugar and continue stirring gently until sugar has dissolved. Continue the low boil, stirring occasionally until marmalade is well-reduced and forms a firm jelly when tested.

Begin to test the marmalade 30 minutes after the sugar has been added. Test either with a cooking thermometer (should reach 225°F) or with a spoon (marmalade should 'sheet' when a small quantity is poured off the side of a spoon).

When the correct stage has been reached, turn off burner and stir in Scottish Highland Liqueur. Let marmalade sit for 10 minutes before ladling into hot, sterilized jelly jars; seal.

INDEX

BASICS OF LIQUEUR MAKING 7
  Aging 14
  Brand Names 15
  Equipment 8
  Ingredients 10
  Siphoning 14

BEVERAGES, COLD
  Adult Milkshake 49
  American Whiskey Punch 51
  Bitter Lemon Highball 47
  Fizzes 48
  Liqueur Frappe 47
  Liqueurs on Ice 46
  Sangria 52
  Thor's Thunder Punch 52

BEVERAGES, HOT
  Dutch 'Anijs Melk' 51
  English Hot Grog 49
  Hot Elizabethan Posset 50
  Liqueur Coffees 46
  Liqueur Hot Chocolate 47

BREADS AND SPREADS
  French Country Pate 58
  Golden Cream 62
  Newfie Girdle Cake With Kummel Butter ... 64
  Seasoned Melba Toast 58
  Whipped Liqueur Butter 65

COOKIES AND CANDY
  Italian Anise Stars 85
  Mocha Truffles 84

DESSERTS
  Almond Tea Cake 68
  Apple Pie Snack Cake 70
  Chocolate-Lover's Cookie Piecrust 80
  Chocolate Nut Ruffle 75
  Danish Fruit Soup 86
  Devonshire Hazelnut Roll 71
  Dutch Lawyers' Pie 76
  Elegant Chocolate Crepes 67
  Fudge Sauce 81
  Ice Cream Social Pie 80
  Irish Cream Cups 78
  Liqueur Glaze 63
  Steamed Orange Pudding 87
  Tristy's Terrific 'Triffle' 73
  Tropicale Yogurt Pie w/Green Butterflies 82
  Vanilla Sugar 88
  Whipped Liqueur Cream 83

EQUIVALENT LIQUID MEASUREMENTS 15

INTRODUCTION 5

LIQUEURS
  Advocaat 19
  Amaretto 30
  Anisette 31
  Appel Liqueur 26
  California Lemon Liqueur 36
  Creme de Cacao 21
  Creme de Menthe 23
  Creme de Prunelle 25
  Danish Cherry Liqueur 18
  Dutch Chocolate-Mint Liqueur 20
  English Damson Plum Liqueur 20
  Fresh Mint Liqueur 22
  Grand Orange-Cognac Liqueur 24
  H & C's Irish Cream 29
  Hawaiian Fruit Liqueur 37
  Italian Gold Liqueur 32
  Italian Hazelnut Liqueur 34
  Kummel Liqueur 27

```
    Mexican Coffee Liqueur ..................  39
    Nassau Vanilla Liqueur ..................  40
    Old Jamaican Coffee Liqueur .............  44
    Orange Curacao ..........................  42
    Ouzo ....................................  28
    Pina Colada Liqueur .....................  41
    Scottish Highland Liqueur ...............  35
    Taboo Liqueur ...........................  38

MAIN DISHES/CASSEROLES
    German Appel Pancake Puff ...............  66
    Hint O' Mint Lamb Chops and Stuffing ....  57
    Mandarin Yam Bake .......................  63

MAKING LIQUEURS ............................  17

PRESERVES AND SAUCES
    California Lemon Sauce ..................  60
    Fudge Sauce .............................  81
    Highland Marmalade ......................  89
    Oriental Plum Sauce .....................  61

SERVING LIQUEURS ...........................  46

SOUPS
    Danish Fruit Soup .......................  86
    International Cheese Soup ...............  59
```